Master Meditation and The Law of Attraction

Introduction to Meditation, Hypnosis & Affirmation Techniques to Learn the Secret of Attracting Wealth, Health, Love, Success, Positivity and More!

Olivia Clifford

© **Copyright 2021 - All rights reserved.**

The content contained within this book may not be reproduced, duplicated or transmitted without direct written permission from the author or the publisher.

Under no circumstances will any blame or legal responsibility be held against the publisher, or author, for any damages, reparation, or monetary loss due to the information contained within this book, either directly or indirectly.

Legal Notice:

This book is copyright protected. It is only for personal use. You cannot amend, distribute, sell, use, quote or paraphrase any part, or the content within this book, without the consent of the author or publisher.

Disclaimer Notice:

Please note the information contained within this document is for educational and entertainment purposes only. All effort has been executed to present accurate, up to date, reliable, complete information. No warranties of any kind are declared or implied. Readers acknowledge that the author is not engaged in the rendering of legal, financial, medical or professional advice. The content within this book has been derived from various sources. Please consult a licensed professional before attempting any techniques outlined in this book.

By reading this document, the reader agrees that under no circumstances is the author responsible for any losses, direct or indirect, that are incurred as a result of the use of the information contained within this document, including, but not limited to, errors, omissions, or inaccuracies.

Table of contents

INTRODUCTION

CHAPTER 1: THE LAW OF ATTRACTION

MINDFULNESS

Using the Law of Attraction

Visualization

CHAPTER 2: MEDITATION AND HYPNOSIS

Meditation

Hypnosis

Myths About Hypnosis

Self-Hypnosis

CHAPTER 3: AFFIRMATIONS

The Importance of Touch

Designing Affirmations

Examples of Affirmations

Powerful Affirmations for Love

Powerful Affirmations for Financial Success

Powerful Affirmations for Weight Loss

Powerful Affirmations for Relationships

Powerful Affirmations for Happiness

CHAPTER 4: BREATHING

The Process of Breathing

Deep Breathing

Alternate Nostril Breathing

Humming & Bumble Bee Breath

CHAPTER 5: GUIDED MEDITATION FOR THE LAW OF ATTRACTION

A Beginner's Guide to Meditation

Meditation for Love

Meditation for Money

Meditation for Happiness

Meditation for Weight Loss

CHAPTER 6: GUIDED HYPNOSIS FOR THE LAW OF ATTRACTION

A Beginner's Guide to Hypnosis

Hypnosis for Love

Hypnosis for Money

Hypnosis for Happiness

Hypnosis for Weight Loss

CONCLUSION

REFERENCES

Introduction

"Your calm mind is the ultimate weapon against your challenges" - Bryant McGill (Goodreads, n.d.-a).

There are a few terms that you must define for yourself before beginning your practice.

1. Happiness

The Merriam-Webster dictionary defines *happiness* as a state of well-being and contentment and goes further to list synonyms including blessedness, bliss, gladness, joy, and warm fuzzies (Merriam-Webster, n.d.-a)

Although happiness can be defined by the terms mentioned above, it's important to acknowledge the subjectiveness of it all. A lunch outing with your family could bring you an immense feeling of happiness and joy, while someone else might find their family unbearable, and spending time with them might bring that person unhappiness and despair. Many people describe happiness as being satisfied with life or the feeling of positive emotions, but it's also important to acknowledge that you can live a happy life while still experiencing moments of sadness.

You see, happiness and sadness go hand in hand. If you've never experienced sadness, then how would you know when the sadness no longer lingers and when happiness creeps in?

I'm sure you've heard the phrase "happiness comes from within," which ties the feeling of happiness with self-confidence, self-belief, self-esteem, and self-image. In addition, many psychologists suggest that being happy is a choice that you can control with your perception of situations and how you respond in these situations (Ackerman, 2019).

These are some of the aspects that you'll learn to focus on when meditating for a greater sense of happiness, but before you can begin, make sure that you know what happiness means to you or at least have a general idea.

When defining happiness for yourself, focus on your intention. A positive intention has been shown to bring more happiness than simply wanting more. Let's break this down a little. If you've decided that buying that multimillion-dollar house will bring you happiness and you want to meditate on this idea, ask yourself why you think this will bring you happiness before beginning your meditation. What is your intention behind buying this house? Do you want the house because you feel like your family deserves it after standing by you through thick and thin? Do you feel like they will have a better quality of life in this setting or do you want the house to drop it in conversation and flaunt the fact that you can afford it? The intention behind your actions, aspirations, and goals are vital when applying the law of attraction, which is outlined in the first chapter. Having positive and good intentions that will positively impact the lives of others and are known to have more positive outcomes and be more sustainable (Kirk, 2019).

While talking about intention, let's quickly cover the topic of money.

The guided meditation and affirmations in this book are based on the law of attraction. Once again, your intention behind meditating to improve your financial success should be defined before your practice. The more positive your intentions, the more positive the outcome of your practice. Now, it's important to realize that meditating to increase financial success won't make you a billionaire overnight. Neither will meditating for love bring you a lover, nor meditating for weight loss make you thinner in a week. Meditation and hypnosis work on one's self to increase personal development and growth so that your goals and aspirations become more attainable as time goes by.

2. Wealth

The Merriam-Webster dictionary defines wealth as an abundance of valuable material possessions or resources (Merriam-Webster, n.d.-c).

Once again, the subjectiveness of wealth is important. A man living in a two-bedroom house with his wife and two daughters can have all the wealth that he desires while a man living in a mansion with his wife and son can be constantly searching for more. When using the law of attraction and meditation for wealth, it is important, once again, to define your intention behind your desire.

3. Well-Being

According to the Merriam-Webster dictionary, well-being refers to a state of being happy, healthy, or prosperous. (Merriam-Webster, n.d.-d)

When usually thinking of health, the absence of illness comes to mind. Someone who is physically able, strong, and well-looking is said to be in good health, but this is a common misconception.

You see, the World Health Organization (WHO) defined health as "a state of complete physical, mental and social well-being and not merely the absence of disease or infirmity" (WHO, 2019).

This definition was adopted in 1948 and has not been amended since, although there has been talk of the addition of economic or financial well-being to the definition. So, from this definition, it is possible to conclude that mental and social well-being play just as big a role in health as the physical aspect.

With this in mind, a physically disabled man with an amputated leg, unable to move without the aid of his wheelchair, could have a great level of mental and social health and still live a happy and healthy life. This man could be said to be healthier than the old lady a couple of doors away who looks physically fit but lacks the coping mechanisms to deal with her rude daughter-in-law and has recently shied away from social interaction with her friends for the same reason.

4. Love

The Merriam-Webster dictionary defines love as a strong affection for another arising out of kinship or personal ties, affection based on admiration, common interests, or attraction based on sexual desires (Merriam-Webster, n.d.-b)

When it comes to any relationship, be it romantic, family, or friends, it's usually easier to find fault in the other person when something goes wrong. The meditation techniques using the law of affirmation that are outlined in this book describes the importance of self-reflecting and being true to yourself when interacting with others. It's important to ensure that you're ready for a relationship before diving into one headfirst, whether it's a new friendship or more romantic. Family relationships are usually much more difficult to deal with while it's easy to simply run away from people you don't have blood ties with. That's where meditation and the power of calming your mind comes in!

Now that you've got a general understanding of the definitions above, let's get into it!

Chapter 1: The Law of Attraction

"Once you make a decision, the universe conspires to make it happen" - Ralph Waldo Emerson (Ralph Waldo Emerson Quotes, n.d.-a).

Basically, the law of attraction states that you'll attract into your life what you focus on. Whatever you put your energy into will manifest and come back to you in a positive way.

The widely accepted dogma in the law of attraction is that "like attracts like." Let me break it down for you.

The law of attraction is based on energy, focus, and intention. Positive energy is associated with feelings, thoughts, and actions that are positive. This may include feelings of happiness, joy, compassion, and gratitude. Thoughts that bring about these feelings as well as those that draw your focus to your goals and the things that are important to you are also positive. Lastly, your actions that are in keeping with your positive thoughts and feelings are naturally positive. Generally, positivity is associated with good.

Any of your thoughts, actions, and feelings that give you a sense of happiness and positivity, usually work *for* you in building your life and give you a positive sense of well-being. Thoughts, actions, and feelings that work *against* you in achieving your goals and aspirations are usually classified as "bad" and are associated with negative energy. For example, consistent thoughts of anger, lashing out at the people you love, or even snoozing that alarm clock one too many times every morning could be a few examples. Anger always leaves you feeling worse than you started, and lashing out at the ones you love makes everyone unhappy. These things work *against* you in building a happy life of positive well-being. Snoozing that alarm clock one too many times, although a meager action compared to the anger, also works *against* you in building your life because it allows you to slip into the bad habit of waking up late which will then impact your punctuality, leading to a bad professional reputation and maybe eventually make you unemployable. I know this seems a little extreme, but that's what happens when you let negative energy and bad habits grow out of control like that.

The energy that you give out is the energy that you'll receive. Now, this book is written in the context of living a happier and healthier life and using the law of attraction to help you reach your aspirations and build a life of happiness and positive well-being. Of course, there is no light without the dark, so there is no positivity without negativity, and each has its part to play. Negative feelings and thoughts can't be banished, never to be seen or heard of again, but the way you react to these feelings and thoughts can be positive and is very much in your control.

Positive energy attracts positive energy; negative energy attracts negative energy. Have you ever noticed how one success usually spearheads a whole series of successes and victories? That, my friend, is the law of attraction. The initial success left you feeling so positive and inspired that you began emitting a sense of positivity that the universe responded to, sending more positivity your way! What about the way anger or fear seems to compound in certain situations? Again, you begin emitting a negative energy that attracts more negativity toward yourself.

This means that you can manifest certain aspirations or outcomes by having positive intentions and practicing techniques that allow you to experience and emit more positivity. Whatever energy you're creating will determine how the universe responds to you and the opportunities that will present themselves to you.

Whatever you're thinking, feeling, and doing at any given time creates vibrations in the form of energy that will attract the energy of the same frequency i.e., positive or negative (Canfield, 2019).

Knowing that you're mostly in control of the energy you emit is not enough to use the power of the law of attraction to your advantage. In addition to your energy frequencies and intentions being in tune with your system of values and beliefs, you need to also consciously create a better life for yourself in the process. You can do this by:

- Choosing how to react in certain situations
- Choosing to challenge your thoughts that bring about negative emotions and feelings
- Choosing to spend your time doing things that make you happy and feel positive
- Choosing to adjust your lifestyle and habits so that they are in keeping with your intentions, values, and beliefs
- Choosing to be open-minded and objective when the situation calls for it
- Choosing to practice gratitude and focusing on all that you have instead of all that you don't have

The process of consciously creating a better life for yourself requires a well-known practice called mindfulness which goes hand-in-hand with meditation and positive living.

Mindfulness

"The present moment is the only time over which we have dominion. Live the actual moment. Only this actual moment is life" - Thich Nhat Hanh (Goodreads, n.d.-b).

Mindfulness is the ability to be fully present and aware of your internal and external environments. Your internal environment includes your thoughts, feelings, and emotions, all of which you have a certain degree of control over. This environment also includes your perceptions and perspectives, your opinions, and the choices you make before you carry out your actions. Your external environment refers to the things around you that you have no control over. These include other people's opinions, the weather, the traffic, the stock markets, and the like. You do, however, have control of how to respond to situations in your external environment, and this makes all the difference.

Practicing mindfulness will allow you to identify experiences that leave with negative feelings and thus attracting more negativity. This way, you can modify these experiences to make them more positive or even avoid these experiences altogether. Let's look at a simple example. Your wife insists that you go out with all of her friends' husbands for a guy's night once a month. The day arrives, and there are four of you in total. You have nothing in common with the other husbands, and although you try to involve yourself in the conversation, it feels forced and inorganic. You feel a sense of pressure and anxiety when interacting with them, and you can tell that they feel it, too. Being mindful of your thoughts, feelings, and body language in this situation will tell you that the energy you're emitting is not exactly positive. You're anxious, a little on edge, annoyed that you're unable to hold a decent conversation, and a little stressed because you really want to make this work to make your wife happy. At the end of the experience, you head home and assess the night. The truth is, you had a terrible time, and you would have been much happier just staying home and spending time with your wife. That would have improved your mood and conversation and you would have felt more comfortable, resulting in an overall positive experience. Now you have to decide whether it's in the best interest of you and your wife if you continue to go out with the guys once a month.

Worst-case scenario is that you'll keep going out with them, and slowly but surely you would begin to resent your wife for forcing you to do it in the first place. Best case-scenario is that you sit down and have a conversation with your wife about the fact that you tried but you just don't feel comfortable going out with those guys every month. It isn't anything they did or said, they just aren't your type of people, and that's okay. Then, you might end up using that time to attend a monthly cooking class with your wife which will leave you feeling happy and fulfilled, and it will positively influence your sense of well-being.

When aiming to live a more positive life, it's important to still remember that negative experiences have their place, and sometimes discomfort is required for growth. Being mindful should also come with complete honesty with yourself about your experiences. Let's take learning how to swim, for example. You may feel like you're drowning sometimes and a sense of complete discomfort in the icy water, but keeping in mind the intention behind the experience can help you maintain a positive mindset that will counteract these experiences. For example, you may say to yourself, "It might feel like I'm drowning sometimes, but not for much longer. Soon I'll be able to swim!" or even "The water may be icy, but these few moments of discomfort are worth me learning how to swim!"

Using the Law of Attraction

The energy that you emit comes from your thoughts, feelings, and actions, so every moment of every day there are vibrations that are being sent out from your being. To control your mind every second of every day would be an extremely taxing process, and the focus required will prevent you from living life to the fullest. It is important not to become obsessive about your thoughts and feelings. You'll find that small everyday changes, like those described in a later chapter, can positively impact the way you experience life and when regularly practiced can become somewhat of a habit.

First things first, when using the law of attraction to reach your goals and aspirations, it's important to be intentional about them. Clearly define your goal and the reason you want to achieve it. Then ask yourself the following questions:

1. Why do I want to achieve my goal?
2. What are the steps I need to take to get closer to this goal?
3. How long do I think it will take me to achieve this goal?
4. Once I achieve this goal, how do I intend to sustain it?

Be completely honest with yourself when asking these questions. Once you have defined your goal and the intention behind it, you may start your visualization process.

Visualization

"Visualization is daydreaming with a purpose" - Bo Bennett (Bo Bennett Quotes, n.d.).

Visualization techniques are essential in using the law of attraction to achieve your goals. Being able to see or imagine your aspirations within reach will keep you inspired and motivated as well as allow you to emit positive energy.

You may visualize yourself achieving your goal and imagine the feelings and emotions that will come with the achievement. Imagine the exact scene from the clothes that you're wearing to the people you want to share the moment with.

Creating a vision board that you can display in a visible area will also remind you of your goals and the positive feelings that it brings. However, visualizing the end goal is just as important as visualizing how to get there.

Focus on and talk about or journal what you want to manifest your goals. Don't focus on what you don't want! Maintain a sense of positivity and inspiration by remembering your intention behind the goal.

After you have an idea about how to go about achieving your goal and you've been focusing on what you want to achieve in a positive light, take action to bring you closer to your aspiration. Remember, the law of attraction doesn't work if you don't! Believe that you're going to achieve your goals and understand that if you don't, it means that there was something better meant for you.

Attach positive emotions and feelings to your goals and aspirations and set yourself daily reminders to journal or even just think about what you wish to achieve. Speak these thoughts into the universe to manifest your goals while taking action to achieve them.

As Ralph Waldo Emerson said, "A man is what he thinks about all day long." (Ralph Waldo Emerson Quotes, n.d.-b).

Chapter 2: Meditation and Hypnosis

Meditation

"Learn to be calm and you will always be happy" - Paramahansa Yogananda ("Learn to be calm and you will always be happy," n.d.).

Meditation is a daily practice that allows you to sit quietly and still your mind so that you may experience a sense of calm and relaxation. There are various techniques and ways in which you can meditate, but ultimately, the goal of meditation is to nourish the mind like we nourish the body: daily.

Throughout our lives, we are constantly moving, both body and mind, and focusing on getting from one place to the next. Be it getting from home to work or maybe getting from working as an assistant to working as a manager, the point is, we are constantly looking to where we can go next. Meditation is a practice that allows you to be still and, at the moment, as you slow down a little and be mindful of all that you have, while still giving some attention to what you wish to accomplish.

Mindfulness meditation, originating from Buddhist teachings, is the most commonly practiced form of meditation in the Western world and incorporates being completely aware of your body, mind, and external environment as you repeat a mantra, allowing your mind to settle and be completely present in the moment.

Meditative practices have been shown to improve daily focus, reduce anxiety, increase creativity, improve memory and cognitive functioning, as well as increase compassion and feelings of positivity among individuals (Cooper, 2013).

The use of meditation in the achievement of goals and aspirations has been practiced for centuries. Being mindful of your intentions and aspirations during the meditative process has been associated with feelings of positivity and calm that contribute to the positive energy that is emitted from an individual.

Hypnosis

"The easier you can make it inside your head, the easier it will make things outside your head" - Richard Bandler (n.d.).

More commonly, "hypnosis is a state of extreme self-focus and attention in which minimal attention is given" to the external environment, unlike in meditation where the external environment is observed as well (Lumen, n.d.). This trance-like state showcases heightened focus and concentration and leaves the individual in a suggestible mood. Being open to suggestions can help you gain control of undesirable behaviors as well as allow you to consider changes in your lifestyle that may benefit you positively (Mayo Clinic, 2018).

Myths About Hypnosis

There are a few myths and misunderstandings associated with hypnosis and hypnotherapy that are important to iron out before going any further (HMI College of Hypnotherapy, 2004):

1. Hypnosis involves mind control.

This is absolutely incorrect! No one can control your mind unless you let them. Hypnosis simply induces a suggestible state that will allow your mind to be more open to changes that will positively influence your well-being. Your subconscious mind will reject all suggestions that you don't agree with or don't understand. You can specify exactly what suggestions you want your hypnotherapist to feed your superconscious mind while being hypnotized.

2. Hypnosis will allow someone else to control my body.

Once again, not true! This assumption is based on Hollywood fiction, mostly. Although your mind is in a suggestible state, allowing yourself to partake in serious suggestions about your self-improvement will not leave you barking like a dog or walking like a duck.

3. If I can be hypnotized, it means that my mind is weak.

This belief, although common throughout most of history, has actually been scientifically proven as untrue. The most important aspect of hypnotism is the willingness to be induced into a suggestible state of mind. Going into a hypnotherapist's room with a closed mind is not going to give you the results you desire. Even war veterans, who have been trained in the psychology of killing and have the mental strength exceed that of an average civilian, have been hypnotized in the treatment of post-traumatic stress disorder (PTSD).

4. If I'm hypnotized, I will have no memory of it.

Hypnosis is not an unconscious state of sleep; it's actually associated with hyperawareness, heightened concentration and focus, and increased sensitivity of the senses.

5. I might not be able to snap out of it if I'm hypnotized.

Coming out of hypnosis is similar to coming out of meditation, to be quite honest. Simply stretching or gently opening your eyes can naturally allow you to transcend out of the hypnotic state.

6. Hypnosis will cause amnesia.

Only a very small percentage of people who undergo hypnosis go into a deep enough level or state that may cause spontaneous amnesia. The vast majority of individuals remember everything from their hypnotic experiences and may even experience enhancements in memory.

Self-Hypnosis

Self-hypnosis, involving no external party, like the guide provided in this book, is significantly more affordable than a weekly hypnotherapist appointment and can provide very similar results. In addition, you have access to the guide whenever you need it and can practice as often as you like in the comfort and privacy of your own home.

Although the self-hypnosis guide in this book is a general guide that can be modified as specified, it is also possible for you to adopt the guide to other specific issues that you may require help with. There is an additional guideline on how to adapt the guide to other specific issues included at the end of the guided hypnosis chapter.

Since with self-hypnosis, there is no second party involved, it is important to journal the thoughts and emotions that may arise during your hyperaware state and analyze these thoughts and emotions at a later stage. These analyses may bring to light other issues that may need some attention (St John, 2018).

The more you practice the technique of self-hypnosis, the easier it will become to reach the hypnotic state.

Chapter 3: Affirmations

Affirmations are positive phrases or words that can help you overcome natural negativity and negative thoughts. In addition, these statements can keep you motivated, inspired, and promote an overall feeling of positivity (Mind Tools, 2019).

According to a study done on positive thinking, spending just a few minutes thinking about your positive characteristics and reminding yourself how capable you are and can significantly improve your performance and problem-solving abilities (Kang et al., 2015).

Affirmations and positive self-talk have also recently been used to successfully treat people with low self-esteem and depression, resulting in positive therapeutic outcomes and overall improved quality of life (Peden et al., 2001).

Words have immense power, and affirmations and positive self-talk can positively affect your life by:

- Motivating and inspiring you to put your plans into action
- Helping you remain focused on your goals
- Boosting your self-confidence and self-belief
- Helping improve and maintain relationships
- Improving health and well-being

All of these positive effects essentially improve your energy frequency which results in the emission of positive energy. This in turn, by the law of attraction, results in an increased chance of success and achievement.

The Importance of Touch

Scientific research undertaken on the importance of touch and the effect it has on the human body has shown that touch expresses warmth, trust, and mostly positive emotions (Schwartz, 2016).

The research has shown that basic warm touch calms cardiovascular stress, even when one uses their own palms to warm their own shoulders. When stressed or sad, you might find yourself curling up into the fetal position on your bed, rocking your body back and forth. Researchers suggest that this position is ideal for stress management, as it allows most of your body to be in contact with another part, spreading the warmth and the feeling of safety.

In the same way, while practicing aspirations, patting your chest or touching your forehead can increase the positive experience of this practice. For example, sit comfortably and gently close your eyes. Once your eyes are closed, breathe in and out, simply calming your mind. Then start to say your affirmation out loud. While you say your affirmation, bring one of your palms to your chest and gently pat your chest. Pat your chest as you repeat, "I love myself because I am me".

Designing Affirmations

Now that you have an understanding of what affirmations are, let's have a look at how to design your own affirmations that are specific to you.

A couple of tips when designing affirmations are as follows:

1. Always create the affirmation in the present tense. Starting with the words, "I am" is usually a good way to go.
2. Always state the affirmation in a positive way. For example, instead of, "I am not weak and scared," rather say, "I am strong and courageous."
3. Make your affirmations specific to your goals. For example, if your goal is to be a world-class swimmer you might say, "I will swim 50 meters in under 25 seconds."
4. If you find yourself stuck at a negative thought, use the word "but" to change the narrative. For example, "I am overweight

and struggling with my exercise routine, but I am still here, and I am still trying."

Remember, using the law of attraction and positivity will not have you achieving your goals overnight. You still need to work for what you want to achieve!

Examples of Affirmations

Although this book contains guided meditations and hypnosis for love, money, weight loss, relationships, and happiness, there are many other aspects of your life that you can assess and address with meditation and hypnosis to ultimately experience positive outcomes.

Affirmations come into play during the meditation or hypnosis where you may want to repeat them as mantras or even just as daily reminders or inspiration.

Now, as mentioned earlier in this book, self-development and self-awareness are both a large part of living happy and healthy. Looking to develop one's self instead of looking externally to blame others for negative experiences is a large part of the growth process and can positively impact your well-being and quality of life. As a result, each of the following sections will also contain affirmations aimed at you, the individual, and your self-development.

Powerful Affirmations for Love

1. I deserve to find love.
2. My heart is open for love.
3. I have more love to give than I ever thought possible.
4. I am surrounded by love.

5. I love my spouse.
6. I deserve to be loved the way my spouse loves me.
7. My love is unconditional.
8. I love without restraint.
9. Someone out there deserves my love.
10. I will find the one who deserves my love.
11. I am attracting love.
12. I have love within me.
13. I am grateful for the love that I have.
14. The more I love myself, the more I love my partner.
15. I deserve happiness.
16. I am open to love.
17. I give and receive love.
18. I believe in my ability to love.
19. When I am ready for love, love will find me.
20. I am thankful that the universe will help me find love.
21. I will allow love to find me easily.
22. I am ready for love to find me.
23. I can love, so I can be loved.
24. I trust my partner completely.
25. I let love flow into my life.
26. I am building my life with love.
27. I share my life with my love.
28. Life is full of love.
29. I will be my true love's love.
30. I will attract my best friend in a lover.

Powerful Affirmations for Financial Success

1. Money flows toward me.
2. I am worthy of the money that is coming my way.
3. There is always more than enough money in my life.
4. I deserve to be paid for my skills.
5. I am wealthy in so many ways.
6. I am grateful for the abundance of wealth that I possess.
7. I am worthy of the richness I desire.
8. I am aligned with my purpose.
9. What's meant for me is coming.

10. I am aligned with the energy of abundance.
11. I will boldly conquer my financial goals.
12. I humbly accept and receive the money that is coming toward me.
13. I am growing into someone who is financially successful.
14. I am learning the skills required to make me financially successful.
15. I am in control of my success.
16. I will be successful, maybe not immediately but indefinitely.
17. I am responsible for my financial success.

Powerful Affirmations for Weight Loss

1. I deserve good health.
2. I am going to lose weight and achieve my goals.
3. I am listening to what my body needs from me.
4. I am pushing my body to its limits.
5. I am transforming my lifestyle into something healthier.
6. I am making small and sustainable changes that will benefit me in the long run.
7. I feel happier and healthier.
8. I am active and full of energy.
9. I choose to nourish my body in a healthy way.
10. I am fitter today than I was yesterday.
11. I nourish my body with what I feed it.
12. I think before I eat.
13. I am moving forward each day.
14. I breathe in relaxation and breathe out stress.
15. I am drinking water to regulate my mood and metabolism.
16. I crave mindfulness more than I crave sweet treats.
17. I am on a path of wellness.
18. I love my body.
19. I value self-control and self-mastery.
20. I will control my impulses and cravings.
21. I wake up each day with determination.
22. I strengthen my own self-mastery by resisting temptation.
23. I am strong enough to achieve this goal.
24. I acknowledge that not all thoughts need to be acted on.

25. I challenge my existing beliefs.
26. I make peace with the past.
27. I find new hope in every new day.
28. I am capable of discipline.
29. I am healthy.
30. I can lose weight easily.
31. I am patient with myself and my body.

Powerful Affirmations for Relationships

1. I am surrounded by love and acceptance.
2. I love and accept those around me.
3. I attract good, kind, and loving people into my life.
4. I welcome kindness and love with open arms.
5. I appreciate all the people I have in my life.
6. My partner and I love each other.
7. My partner and I laugh every day.
8. I feel happy in my partner's presence.
9. Our love is stronger than arguments.
10. Love always wins.
11. I go through life with the help of my loved ones.
12. I am ready to accept a happy, fulfilling relationship.
13. I deserve the happiness that my loved ones bring me.
14. I love myself to the fullest.
15. Love is all around me, and I am worthy of it.
16. I am surrounded by love.
17. I attract loving people into my life because I am loving.
18. I appreciate all that I am.
19. I am good enough the way I am.
20. I am still growing and changing as time goes by.
21. I am becoming better for the ones that I love.
22. I am working on being able to communicate more openly.
23. I will be able to communicate more openly.
24. I am nonjudgmental toward others just as I am toward myself.
25. I release all desperation and allow love to find me.

Powerful Affirmations for Happiness

1. I have the power to shape my ideal reality.
2. I create the life I want with my good intentions.
3. When I feel happy, I manifest more reasons to be happy.
4. I am happy right now.
5. I am worthy of feeling happy.
6. My happiness comes from within me.
7. There are so many positives in my life.
8. I am so grateful for the happiness that I have.
9. I experience so much joy in the things that I do.
10. I allow myself to feel happy and good.
11. My choice to be happy keeps me healthy.
12. I am meant to live a happy life.
13. My inner joy overflows into my life and allows me to share this feeling with others.
14. I am grateful to be alive.
15. Happiness is my birthright.
16. Good things are happening within me and around me.
17. I feel deeply fulfilled.

Chapter 4: Breathing

The Process of Breathing

When you breathe in or inhale, the muscle just beneath your ribcage, your diaphragm, contracts and moves downward, allowing your lungs more space to expand. The muscles between your ribs, known as your intercostal muscles, contract and push your ribcage upward and outward. As your lungs expand, air travels down your trachea from your nose and your mouth and eventually reaches your lungs. When the air has reached the little air sacs at the end of its journey into your lungs, oxygen from the air you have breathed passes into the bloodstream. At the same time, carbon dioxide passes from your bloodstream into your lungs and is exhaled and released from the body (Elliot, 2017).

Every process in the body relies on oxygen. Your organs need ample oxygen to function properly, so effective breathing can increase your digestion, improve your body's immunity, improve your cognition and memory, and even help you sleep better (Elliot, 2017).

During meditation and when inducing hypnosis, focusing on your breath is important to help you reach a deeper state of consciousness. Different breathing techniques exist that may be practiced with meditation or in isolation, with different benefits in daily life. A few of the techniques are mentioned in this chapter.

Deep Breathing

In everyday life, the shallow breaths that we take while carrying out everyday tasks allow us to take in enough oxygen to ensure that our body and mind are functional. Even though something is functioning doesn't mean that it is functioning optimally or to the best of its ability. Utilizing certain breathing techniques can improve the functionality of the body and mind. Deep breathing is one of these techniques.

Deep breathing, or diaphragmatic breathing, is a technique that is practiced widely with meditation. It focuses on slowing down your breathing and being mindful of the air as it enters and leaves your body.

The benefits of deep breathing or diaphragmatic breathing have been studied in-depth and include (Jewell, 2018):

- Lowering levels of the stress hormone cortisol in your body, thus increasing relaxation
- Improving core muscle stability and balance
- Improving cognitive function and memory
- Improving immunity against infection
- Increasing and improving digestion
- Stimulating the lymphatic system to remove excess toxins from the body
- Increasing energy
- Reducing blood pressure and heart rate

Before getting into a deep breathing exercise, you must practice this technique on an empty stomach or about an hour after a meal. Eating a large meal before practicing can make you feel uncomfortable.

Let's practice deep breathing!

Sit in a comfortable seated position with your back straight. If you're a beginner and are unable to sit cross-legged for long periods, don't beat yourself up: You'll get there if that's what you want. Rather, sit on a chair with a backrest so that your back remains upright to allow for the expansion of your lungs. Allow your hands to gently fall in your lap and close your eyes.

First, breathe in, completely, sucking in as much air as you can through your nose, to the count of three. As you breathe in, expand your chest by sticking it outward and swell out your tummy, allowing your lungs to inflate completely. Be mindful of the breath as it enters your body. Feel the air enter your nose and flow down into your lungs. Notice the temperature of the air as it enters your body. Hold the breath in your lungs for a moment and then slowly breathe out, through your nose or mouth, whichever is more comfortable, to the count of six. While breathing out, ensure that your back remains straight, and as you push all the air out of your lungs, suck in your tummy, feeling your abdominal muscles working as you do. As soon as all the air has been pushed out of your lungs, take a nice deep breath in again, to the count of three. Remember, focus on the breath, feel it going down into your lungs and swell your tummy out to allow your lungs to expand completely, and then hold the breath for a moment. Then slowly release your breath to the count of six, sucking your tummy in to push all the extra air out. Focus on feeling the breath as it enters and leaves your body.

Breathing out for double the count that you breathe in for is an important aspect of deep breathing. This technique stimulates the branch of the nervous system that controls your rest and digest function and therefore improves digestion while allowing you to feel relaxed and rested.

Alternate Nostril Breathing

This type of breath enters and leaves through the nose only and has also shown to have many benefits, including (Art of Living Faculty, 2020):

- Lowering stress and anxiety
- Improving cardiovascular function
- Improving lung capacity
- Improving cognitive function and memory
- Harmonizes the right and left hemispheres of the brain
- Maintains body temperature

Let's breathe!

Sit in a comfortable seated position, once again your back must be straight to allow for maximum expansion of the lungs. Sitting on a chair with a backrest is ideal for beginners. Allow your nondominant hand to gently rest in your lap. If you're right-handed, your left hand will be resting in your lap; if you're left-handed, your right hand will be resting in your lap. In the guide below, the right hand is taken as dominant.

Now, hold your dominant hand in front of you, palm facing you, and fold your middle and pointer finger inward toward your palm. Now, bring your hand to your face and place your index finger over your left nostril and your thumb over your right. Your fingers should be placed so that it is easy to pinch your nose closed.

Close your right nostril with your thumb, releasing your left nostril by lifting your index finger. Breathe in deeply through your left nostril, feeling the breath as it travels down into your lungs, expanding your tummy as you do. When you have taken in as much air as you can, close the left nostril by pinching your nose closed, and hold the breath for a moment. Then, open the right nostril by releasing the thumb and slowly, in a controlled manner, breath out, pushing all the air out of your lungs and sucking your tummy in as you do. While your right nostril is still open, breathe in deeply and completely, feeling the breath in your body and expanding your tummy as you do. Then pinch your nose, closing both nostrils as you hold your breath for a moment. When you're ready to breathe out, release your left nostril by lifting your index finger, and slowly, in a controlled manner, breathe out completely, sucking your tummy in as you do. Then, breathe in through the left nostril again.

Humming & Bumble Bee Breath

This technique allows for the creation of vibrations while exhaling that have been shown to increase nitric oxide (NO) production in the sinuses of the skull. NO from our nose and sinuses is inhaled with every breath we take and works on the blood vessels in the lungs to cause dilation and enhance the body's ability to take up oxygen as well as remove carbon dioxide (Harrold, 2020).

The humming bee breath is a great practice for relaxation and calming as well. The benefits of this technique include (Harrold, 2020):

- Calming the mind
- Boosting the immune system
- Reducing blood pressure
- Regulating metabolism
- Reducing inflammation
- Improving digestion
- Improving memory and decision-making skills

Let's hum like a bee!

Bring yourself into a comfortable seated position with your back straight so that you can expand your lungs completely. Once again, sitting on a chair with a backrest would be perfect. Gently close your eyes, and place your index fingers on your tragus, the cartilage between your ear and your cheek. You may gently rest your face in the palms of your hand to allow your index fingers to rest on the tragus of each ear.

Take a deep breath in, expanding your tummy as you do, feeling the air enter your body. Now, as you breathe out, make a humming sound from your throat while you gently press the tragus of each ear to close the ear. Feel the vibration in your head and the relaxation that comes with it as you breathe out while humming, and suck your tummy in to push all the air out of your lungs. You may repeat this breath as many times as you'd like.

If you're unable to close your ear with your tragus, gently plugging your ear with your index finger works just as well.

Now that we've learned a few breathing techniques, let's meditate!

Chapter 5: Guided Meditation for the Law of Attraction

A Beginner's Guide to Meditation

To start, practice meditating for about 10 minutes a day, then slowly increase the time as you feel comfortable to 10 minutes twice a day. Eventually, you'll find yourself looking forward to your meditation time and may even want to increase it to 20 minutes twice a day.

Sit in a quiet and comfortable space with your back upright and your body relaxed. It's important to be honest with yourself about where you currently are in your journey. You might not be able to sit cross-legged on the floor for long periods, and that's absolutely okay. In order to experience the full benefits of meditation, it's important to be comfortable. Sitting on a chair with a backrest is a great place to start, and as you become more comfortable sitting cross-legged, you may transition into this position as time goes on. Remember, be honest with yourself about your capabilities and your limits. If you find yourself slouching or unable to maintain an upright posture while sitting without a backrest, rather choose to sit on a chair as sitting upright is vital for your lungs to expand to their full capacity. In addition, muscle spasms and cramps can sometimes make it difficult and uncomfortable to meditate if you're unused to sitting in the cross-legged posture for long periods. For this guide, we'll use a chair, but you may feel free to sit in whichever posture you're comfortable in, making sure that your back is straight and upright.

Sit on a chair with your back upright and against the backrest. Place your feet flat on the floor, being mindful not to cross your legs at your ankles or over your knees. Place your hands on your lap with your palms facing up toward the sky. Ensure that your posture is upright and that your chest is open with your eyes looking forward. Your entire body should be relaxed in this posture; there should be no tension in your body. If you're feeling tension in any area, gently stretch that area before meditating to relieve the tension.

Once you're comfortable in your seated position, gently close your eyes and focus on your breath. Breathe in through your nose to the count of three, pushing out your tummy as you inhale, allowing your lungs to expand to full capacity. Feel the air enter your body through your nose, pass through your throat, and down your chest into your lungs. Feel the temperature of the air and the way it cools your nose as it enters your body. Imagine the air as a breath of positivity that you're breathing in to nourish your body. Once your lungs are filled with air, hold the breath for a moment and then gently release the breath through your nose, slowly and in a controlled manner, to the count of six. Push all the air out of your lungs as you suck your tummy in, feeling your abdominal muscles working. As you breathe out, feel the warmth that it brings as you exhale. Feel the air moving as it travels from your lungs up through your chest and throat and through your nose. Imagine that this warm air is like the dark smoke that comes out of a volcano and that you're breathing out all the negativity that has been holding your back. As you sit and focus on your breath, thoughts will come and go. Allow these thoughts to flow by like a river, and simply observe them as they move along. Don't attach a feeling to these thoughts or fixate on any one of them. Simply let them flow.

While sitting in this meditative state and focusing on your breath, you might want to begin thinking of a mantra. Your mantra doesn't have to be religious or spiritual. It can be an affirmation that you want to recite or even words that will improve your mood and sense of well-being like "gratitude" or "happiness." Remember to hold your mantra in your thoughts and not mouth the words physically. Keep your body still and relaxed and focus on your breath.

Your mantra and intentions during your meditation are very important, as these are the things that determine the frequency of energy that you'll emit. In order to emit positive energy so that you may attract the same, your mantra and intentions must in turn be positive. Using meditation and the law of attraction to achieve your goals and aspirations usually has positive outcomes if practiced with the right energy and intention.

When you're ready to end your meditation, let your mantra go, and bring back your focus only to your breath. Sit there for one or two moments and begin to consciously think words of gratitude. You may want to think of phrases such as, "I am grateful for my being" or "I am thankful for all that I am." Then, gently tilt your head downward, bringing your chin to your chest and stretching the back of your neck, as if to bow to the universe. Slowly become aware of your surroundings by wiggling your toes and your fingers. When you're ready, slowly and gently open your eyes and stretch your arms over your head to bring full awareness back to your body.

Meditation for Love

Begin your meditation as laid out in the guide above. Focus on your breath as you sit comfortably; keep your back straight and your eyes gently closed. Breathe in to three counts, feeling the air as it enters your body through your nose and flows into your lungs. Hold the breath for a moment and then slowly exhale, through your nose, in a controlled manner, to the count of six.

As you breathe in, imagine that the air you're breathing is a pink fog that smells like candy floss and rose petals. Feel the air of love enter your body as you inhale. You're attracting love with your intentions and positive energy. Now, as you breathe out, imagine your breath like the smoke of a volcano, breathing out all the negativity that has prevented you from experiencing love in the past. Don't attach emotions to any thoughts that may flow through your mind. Simply focus on your breath and your intention. The universe will bring love to you because of your positive intentions and energy.

As you breathe and focus on your breath, start thinking of an affirmation for love to remind yourself that the law of attraction will bring love to you if you continue with your positive intentions and energy. The affirmation you may want to hold in your mind may be "I am worthy of love" or "I am ready for love." You may want to refer back to the chapter on affirmations and choose one best suited for how you're feeling on this specific day, or you can create your own affirmations or mantras. For example, you might hold the phrase, "Love will come when the time is right" in your mind, and this might become your mantra. Remember, you may change your mantra each time you meditate.

When you're ready to end your meditation, let your mantra flow away and imagine that it is flowing toward the universe so that the universe may understand your intentions. Think thoughts of gratitude such as, "I am grateful that the universe is on my side." Slowly bring your focus back to only your breath. Slowly become aware of your surroundings as you drop your head forward to stretch the back of your neck, bow to the universe, and start to wiggle your toes and fingers. Then when you're ready, gently open your eyes and stretch your arms over your head.

Meditation for Money

Begin your meditation as laid out in the guide above and focus on your breath. As you breathe in, imagine that the air you're breathing is golden and beautiful. Feel the air as it enters your body through your nose and travels to your lungs. Imagine that you're breathing in the wealth that you deserve. As you breathe out, imagine that the air you're exhaling is like the dark ash from a volcano as you breathe out all the negativity within yourself that has held you back from achieving your aspirations. As you sit and breathe, let the thoughts that come to mind flow past like the water in a river. Now begin to think of a mantra or affirmation in your mind. You may want to hold the thought, "All the money that I deserve is on its way to me" or "I am worthy of the wealth that is coming to me." As you repeat this thought in your mind, continue to focus on your breath and your positive intentions behind your aspiration. You're attracting money with your intentions and positive energy.

When you're ready to end your meditation, let your mantra flow away and imagine that it is flowing toward the universe so that the universe may understand your intentions. Think thoughts of gratitude such as, "I am grateful for all that the universe has given me." Slowly bring your focus back to only your breath. Now, become aware of your surroundings as you drop your head forward to stretch the back of your neck, bow to the universe, and start to wiggle your toes and fingers. Then when you're ready, gently open your eyes and stretch your arms over your head.

Meditation for Happiness

Begin your meditation as laid out in the guide above and focus on your breath. As you breathe in, imagine that the air you're breathing is beautifully colored like a rainbow and smells like flowers, freshly baked cookies, and other little things that may make you happy, like your partner's cologne or the smell of your daughter's baby shampoo. Feel the air as it enters your body through your nose and flows into your lungs and imagine the colors from the air radiating from your lungs throughout your body, spreading happiness throughout your being. As you breathe out, imagine that the air you're exhaling is dark ash of all the negativity within you that you're expelling from your being so that what remains is positivity and light. As you sit and focus on your breath, let the thoughts that come flow away, never fixating or attaching emotion to them. Then, as you become comfortable in your breathing, begin to think of a mantra or affirmation with positive energy and the best of intentions. You may want to hold the thought, "I deserve all the happiness that I experience" or "Happiness comes from within me." As you repeat this thought in your mind, continue to focus on your breath and your positive intentions behind your aspiration. You're attracting more happiness to your life with your positive energy and intentions.

When you're ready to end your meditation, let your mantra flow away and imagine that it is flowing toward the universe so that the universe may understand your intentions. Think thoughts of gratitude such as "I am grateful for all that the universe has given me." Slowly bring your focus back to only your breath. Slowly become aware of your surroundings as you drop your head forward to stretch the back of your neck, bow to the universe, and start to wiggle your toes and fingers. Then when you're ready, gently open your eyes and stretch your arms over your head.

Meditation for Weight Loss

When on a weight-loss journey, it often becomes difficult to maintain motivation and follow through with all your plans. Repeating certain affirmations or mantras during your meditative practices can help you build a healthy and happy life as well as maintain your inspiration and motivation.

Begin your meditation as laid out in the guide above and focus on your breath. As you breathe in, imagine that the air you're breathing is like a silver light that inspires you more with every breath. Feel the air as it moves to your lungs and imagine the silver rays radiating from the center of your being to the rest of your body, spreading a feeling of self-love and care. As you breathe out, imagine that the air you're exhaling is dark ash of all the negativity within you that you're expelling from your being, so that all that remains in the here and now is positivity and light. As you sit and breathe, allow the thoughts that come to mind to flow away, simply observing them without attaching any feelings to or fixating on them. As you breathe, begin to think of a mantra or affirmation with positive intentions and energy. You may want to hold the thought, "I am on this journey to become healthier and happier" or "I owe it to myself to become healthier."

When you're ready to end your meditation, let your mantra flow away and imagine that it is flowing toward the universe so that the universe may understand your intentions. Think thoughts of gratitude such as, "I am grateful for the strength and courage that the universe has gifted me." Slowly bring your focus back to only your breath. Slowly become aware of your surroundings as you drop your head forward to stretch the back of your neck, bow to the universe, and start to wiggle your toes and fingers. Then when you're ready, gently open your eyes and stretch your arms over your head.

Chapter 6: Guided Hypnosis for the Law of Attraction

A Beginner's Guide to Hypnosis

The best way to induce hypnosis is by listening to the sound of someone's voice. If you're listening to the audiobook version of this book, then you're all good to go. If you're reading this book, it would be best if you record the session or involve someone close to you to help you reach a hypnotic state. Although trained hypnotherapists are the best people to approach when wanting to reach a hypnotic state, a good friend, your partner or personally recording can help with the induction, simply by narrating the guide below.

Make sure that you clearly explain to the individual inducing your trance your intentions and goals regarding the practice. Give the individual specific phrases, affirmations, or suggestions to feed your hyperaware mind once you're in your hypnotic state. Your helper needs to be able to speak slowly and in a comforting and calming tone.

Let's begin!

Lie down on your back in a comfortable position with your hands placed on your belly, and gaze up toward the ceiling. Focus on a point in the ceiling as you become aware of your breath and gently slow it down. Breathe slowly, still focusing on that point for a few moments. Notice your eyes feeling heavier with every breath; your eyelids struggling to lift back up when you blink. Notice the sense of calm you feel when you blink; your eyelids wanting to stay closed. Your eyes are too heavy to remain open; you may allow them to gently close. Your breath is slow and steady, and your mind is calm. You're simply existing as you are. I am now going to induce the hypnotic state in which you feel happy, calm, relaxed, and at peace.

Imagine yourself in a beautiful little wooden boat floating along a crystal-clear river as you lie there. The sky is a calming blue with not a cloud to be seen, and you feel safe in the little wooden boat. You're becoming calmer and more relaxed with every breath. You can feel the warm breeze of a summer's day and the fresh smell of the grass. As you smell the air, you become more relaxed still, and you allow yourself to go deeper into your trance. It's so easy to be so relaxed, and it feels so good to go deeper and deeper into your trance. As the river flows closer to the sea, you smell the salt in the air which relaxes you more. As you relax, lying in your little wooden boat, a feeling of calm washing over you; you realize how positive, hopeful, and happy you feel. There is another gust of wind that you feel on your skin, and you go deeper into your trance. Every time you feel the wind on your skin, your trance deepens, and you feel more relaxed. You feel the boat underneath you, and you know that you're safe.

You feel happy, relaxed, and calm. You feel the wind on your skin again, allowing you to sink deeper into your trance. There is a light within you that shines on the ones that you love and brings them comfort and joy. Your inner beauty is what has allowed those around you to love you so dearly. You're a positive force of nature. Your intention is pure, and you emit positivity. The universe is working with you to help you achieve all that you want.

***

At this point in hypnosis, it is important to start feeding the person's mind with information and affirmations that will help them achieve their goals and aspirations.

Hypnosis for Love

You love yourself, and that is the most important kind of love. The love and acceptance that you have for yourself will overflow into all aspects of your life and positively influence the lives of others.

You're worthy of being loved, and the love that you're looking for is on its way to you. When you see the person that you love, you'll have the courage to do what must be done so that you may live happily.

Hypnosis for Money

The universe is sending all the wealth that you deserve your way. You're no longer scared to make difficult financial decisions. Every decision that you make will benefit you in one way or another. You're worthy of all the money that is coming your way.

You no longer need to spend money unnecessarily. You can live within your means and still save up for your future. When you spend money unnecessarily, you don't feel happy and fulfilled. Saving money makes you feel happy and fulfilled.

Hypnosis for Happiness

You're happy and relaxed. You realize that you have all the happiness you could ever need. You continue to attract happiness with your positivity and good intentions.

Happiness comes from within you. You choose to be happy by controlling how you respond in certain situations, giving you a sense of calm and peace of mind.

Hypnosis for Weight Loss

You're beautiful and kind. You'll achieve your weight-loss goals and become healthier and happier. You don't need to eat if you're not hungry.

Eating unhealthy foods makes you feel unhappy and uncomfortable. Eating healthy foods makes you feel happy and lighter. Exercising regularly makes you feel more self-confident and makes you happy.

***

You're slowly coming out of your trance. You're slowly becoming aware of your surroundings again. You can wiggle your toes and fingers and feel your body sinking into the couch. You're safe and protected. Slowly open your eyes and look straight ahead when you're ready. Blink a few times to allow your vision to adjust. Now, sit up and stretch your body, bringing full awareness to yourself.

Conclusion

"You cannot dream yourself into a character, you must hammer and forge yourself one" - James Anthony Froude (James Anthony Froude Quotes, n.d.).

With the guided meditations and hypnosis described in this book, you'll be able to bring yourself one step closer to achieving your goals and aspirations.

However, it's important to realize that meditation and hypnosis are not magical solutions to your problems. You can't meditate twice a day, every day, and then sit on the couch for the rest of the time while waiting for the universe to bring you what you desire. Unfortunately, there are no shortcuts in life. Although meditation and hypnosis do work with the law of attraction to draw your aspirations closer to you, nothing in life works unless you do!

Setting clearly defined goals and working toward these goals is a sure way to achieve them. Slap on some positive intentions, appealing to the law of attraction, and you have yourself a winning formula.

The most important aspect of using the law of attraction in life is the intention and energy behind your aspirations and your being. Positive intentions and energy are bound to attract more positivity, and the same goes for negative energy. One of your main goals in the practice of meditation and hypnosis should be to focus on positive living and intentions. In addition, practicing regular self-reflection and assessing whether your thoughts, emotions, and actions are positive or negative can give you a real starting point on what to focus on. Best of luck to you on your journey.

If you enjoyed this book in anyway, an honest review is always appreciated!

References

Ackerman, C. E. (2019, February 16). *What Is Happiness and Why Is It Important? (+ Definition in Psychology)*. PositivePsychology.com. https://positivepsychology.com/what-is-happiness/

American Society of Clinical Hypnosis. (2013). *Myths About Hypnosis*. Www.asch.net. https://www.asch.net/Public/GeneralInfoonHypnosis/MythsAboutHypnosis.aspx

Art of Living Faculty. (2020, March 17). *Alternate Nostril Breathing Benefits | Pranayama*. The Art of Living Retreat Center. https://artoflivingretreatcenter.org/blog/a-breathing-practice-to-calm-soothe-relax/

Bo Bennett Quotes. (n.d.). BrainyQuote.com. Retrieved April 29, 2021, from BrainyQuote.com Web site: https://www.brainyquote.com/quotes/bo_bennett_167549

Canfield, J. (2019, January 2). *Using the Law of Attraction for Joy, Relationships, Money & More [Guide]*. America's Leading Authority on Creating Success and Personal Fulfillment - Jack Canfield. https://www.jackcanfield.com/blog/using-the-law-of-attraction/

Cooper, B. B. (2013, August 21). *What is Meditation & How Does It Affects Our Brains? | Buffer*. Buffer Resources. https://buffer.com/resources/how-meditation-affects-your-brain/

D'Souza, R. (2019, August 29). *Affirmations*. Clinical Hypnotherapy and Stress Management Cardiff. https://www.clinicalhypnotherapy-cardiff.co.uk/affirmations/

Elliot. (2017, September 26). *The Importance of Proper Breathing for Your Overall Health | Elliot*. Elliott Physical Therapy. https://elliottphysicaltherapy.com/importance-proper-breathing-overall-health/#:~:text=The%20Breath%2FHealth%20Connection

Goodreads. (n.d.-a). *A quote from Simple Reminders*. Goodreads. https://www.goodreads.com/quotes/1307115-your-calm-mind-is-the-ultimate-weapon-against-your-challenges.

Goodreads. (n.d.-b). *A quote from The Miracle of Mindfulness*. Goodreads. https://www.goodreads.com/quotes/8207103-the-present-moment-is-the-only-time-over-which-we.

Harrold, E. (2020, October 27). *Health Benefits Of Humming & Bumble Bee Breath*. Ed Harrold. https://www.edharrold.com/post/health-benefits-of-humming-bumble-bee-breath

HMI College of Hypnotherapy. (2004, September 30). *Hypnosis - Dispelling the Top Ten Myths*. Hypnosis.edu. https://hypnosis.edu/articles/myths

https://www.facebook.com/verywell. (2019). *How Meditation Impacts Your Mind and Body*. Verywell Mind. https://www.verywellmind.com/what-is-meditation-2795927

James Anthony Froude Quotes. (n.d.). BrainyQuote.com. Retrieved April 29, 2021, from BrainyQuote.com Web site: https://www.brainyquote.com/quotes/james_anthony_froude_107683

Jewell, T. (2018). *Diaphragmatic Breathing and Its Benefits*. Healthline. https://www.healthline.com/health/diaphragmatic-breathing

Kang, S. K., Galinsky, A. D., Kray, L. J., & Shirako, A. (2015). Power Affects Performance When the Pressure Is On. *Personality and Social Psychology Bulletin*, 41(5), 726–735. https://doi.org/10.1177/0146167215577365

Kirk. (2019, April 7). *Money Meditation Techniques: Guided Meditation to Attract More Wealth*. ABUNDANATION. https://abundanation.com/money-meditation-techniques/

Learn to be calm and you will always be happy. Paramahansa Yogananda Quote. (n.d.). https://quotefancy.com/quote/884648/Paramahansa-Yogananda-Learn-to-be-calm-and-you-will-always-be-happy.

Lumen. (n.d.). *Hypnosis and Meditation | Introduction to Psychology*. Courses.lumenlearning.com. https://courses.lumenlearning.com/wmopen-psychology/chapter/other-states-of-consciousness/#:~:text=Meditation%20is%20the%20act%20of

MayoClinic. (2018). *Hypnosis - Mayo Clinic*. Mayoclinic.org; https://www.mayoclinic.org/tests-procedures/hypnosis/about/pac-20394405

Merriam-Webster. (n.d.-a). Happiness. In *Merriam-Webster.com dictionary*. Retrieved April 29, 2021, from https://www.merriam-webster.com/dictionary/happiness

Merriam-Webster. (n.d.-b). Love. In *Merriam-Webster.com dictionary*. Retrieved April 29, 2021, from https://www.merriam-webster.com/dictionary/love

Merriam-Webster. (n.d.-c). Wealth. In *Merriam-Webster.com dictionary*. Retrieved April 29, 2021, from https://www.merriam-webster.com/dictionary/wealth

Merriam-Webster. (n.d.-d). Well-being. In *Merriam-Webster.com dictionary*. Retrieved April 29, 2021, from https://www.merriam-webster.com/dictionary/well-being

Mind Tools. (2019). *Using Affirmations: – Harnessing Positive Thinking*. Mindtools.com. https://www.mindtools.com/pages/article/affirmations.htm

Mindful. (2018). *Getting Started with Mindfulness - Mindful*. Mindful. https://www.mindful.org/meditation/mindfulness-getting-started/

Peden, A. R., Rayens, M. K., Hall, L. A., & Beebe, L. H. (2001). Preventing depression in high-risk college women: a report of an 18-month follow-up. *Journal of American College Health: J of ACH*, 49(6), 299–306. https://doi.org/10.1080/07448480109596316

Ralph Waldo Emerson Quotes. (n.d.-a). BrainyQuote.com. Retrieved April 29, 2021, from BrainyQuote.com Web site: https://www.brainyquote.com/quotes/ralph_waldo_emerson_383633

Ralph Waldo Emerson Quotes. (n.d.-b). BrainyQuote.com. Retrieved April 29, 2021, from BrainyQuote.com Web site: https://www.brainyquote.com/quotes/ralph_waldo_emerson_108797

Richard Bandler. (n.d.). AZQuotes.com. Retrieved April 29, 2021, from AZQuotes.com Web site: https://www.azquotes.com/quote/703383

Schwartz, A. (2016). *The Importance of Touch - Positive Psychology*. Www.gracepointwellness.org. https://www.gracepointwellness.org/1434-positive-psychology/article/54518-the-importance-of-touch

St John, B. (2018). *Self-Hypnosis Recordings vs Live Hypnotherapy*. SelfHypnosis.com. https://www.selfhypnosis.com/recordings-vs-live-hypnotherapy/#:~:text=The%20more%20you%20experience%20self

WHO. (2019). *Frequently Asked Questions*. Who.int. https://www.who.int/about/who-we-are/frequently-asked-questions

YogicWayOfLife. (2014, April 29). *Bhramari Pranayama - The Humming Bee Breath*. Yogic Way of Life. https://www.yogicwayoflife.com/bhramari-pranayama-the-humming-bee-breath/

www.ingramcontent.com/pod-product-compliance
Lightning Source LLC
Chambersburg PA
CBHW030917080526
44589CB00010B/343